Ready to Learn
Nouns

How To Play

1 Press the Power button to turn the SD-X Reader on or off. The LED will light up when the SD-X Reader is on.

2 Touch the volume buttons found on this page to adjust the volume.

3 Touch words and pictures on the page to hear audio. These icons start the following activities:

 Hear the sentence.

 Hear the word.

 Spell the word.

4 After two minutes of inactivity, the SD-X Reader will beep and go to sleep.

5 If the batteries are low, the SD-X Reader will beep twice and the LED will start blinking. Replace the batteries by following the instructions on the next page. The SD-X Reader uses two AAA batteries.

6 To use headphones or earbuds, plug them into the headphone jack on the SD-X Reader.

Use the SD-X Reader to touch the stickers. All 100 noun stickers play audio!

Volume

Publications International, Ltd.

Battery Information
Includes two replaceable AAA batteries (UM-4 or LR03).

Battery Installation
1. Open battery door with small flat-head or Phillips screwdriver.
2. Install new batteries according to +/- polarity. If batteries are not installed properly, the device will not function.
3. Replace battery door; secure with small screw.

Battery Safety
Batteries must be replaced by adults only. Properly dispose of used batteries. See battery manufacturer for disposal recommendations. Do not dispose of batteries in fire; batteries may explode or leak. Do not mix alkaline, standard (carbon-zinc), or rechargeable (nickel-cadmium) batteries. Do not mix old and new batteries. Only recommended batteries of the same or equivalent type should be used. Remove weakened or dead batteries. Never short-circuit the supply terminals. Non-rechargeable batteries are not to be recharged. Do not use rechargeable batteries. If batteries are swallowed, in the USA, promptly see a doctor and have the doctor phone 1-202-625-3333 collect. In other countries, have the doctor call your local poison control center. This product uses 2 AAA batteries (2 X 1.5V = 3.0 V). Use batteries of the same or equivalent type as recommended. The supply terminals are not to be short-circuited. Batteries should be changed when sounds mix, distort, or become otherwise unintelligible as batteries weaken. The electrostatic discharge may interfere with the sound module. If this occurs, please simply restart the sound module by pressing any key.

In Europe, the dustbin symbol indicates that batteries, rechargeable batteries, button cells, battery packs, and similar materials must not be discarded in household waste. Batteries containing hazardous substances are harmful to the environment and to health. Please help to protect the environment from health risks by telling your children to dispose of batteries properly and by taking batteries to local collection points. Batteries handled in this manner are safely recycled.

Warning: Changes or modifications to this unit not expressly approved by the party responsible for compliance could void the user's authority to operate the equipment.

NOTE: This equipment has been tested and found to comply with the limits for a Class B digital device, pursuant to Part 15 of the FCC Rules. These limits are designed to provide reasonable protection against harmful interference in a residential installation. This equipment generates, uses, and can radiate radio frequency energy and, if not installed and used in accordance with the instructions, may cause harmful interference to radio communications. However, there is no guarantee that interference will not occur in a particular installation. If this equipment does cause harmful interference to radio or television reception, which can be determined by turning the equipment off and on, the user is encouraged to try to correct the interference by one or more of the following measures: Reorient or relocate the receiving antenna. Increase the separation between the equipment and receiver. Connect the equipment into an outlet on a circuit different from that to which the receiver is connected. Consult the dealer or an experienced radio TV technician for help.

Cover illustrated by Olin Kidd

Illustrator: Olin Kidd

Photo credits: Artville; Brand X; Image Club; iStockphoto; Jupiterimages Unlimited; Photodisc; Shutterstock; Thinkstock

Louis Weber, C.E.O., Publications International, Ltd.
7373 North Cicero Avenue
Lincolnwood, Illinois 60712

Ground Floor, 59 Gloucester Place
London W1U 8JJ

Customer Service:
1-888-724-0144 or customer_service@pilbooks.com
www.pilbooks.com

SD-X Interactive is a registered trademark in the United States and Canada.

Manufactured in China.

8 7 6 5 4 3 2 1
ISBN-10: 1-4508-4679-3
ISBN-13: 978-1-4508-4679-0

Airplane I want to get on the **airplane** and fly somewhere fun!

Airport I went to the **airport** and got on an airplane.

Alligator An **alligator** has a lot of sharp teeth.

Alphabet Monkey is learning the letters of the **alphabet.**

Animal An **animal** can be big or small, short or tall.

Arrow An **arrow** points the way to go.

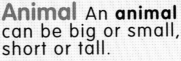

Balloon Hold tight to your **balloon** or it might float away.

Banana I am eating the last **banana**.

Barn Lots of cows live in the **barn**.

Bathtub There is a walrus in my **bathtub**!

Beach I like to watch the waves at the **beach**.

Tell me about the banana again!

Bubble The **bubble** was so pretty until it popped.

Candy It is hard to choose just one piece of **candy**.

Carrot I pretend I'm a bunny when I eat a **carrot**.

This is making me hungry!

Cherry I put a **cherry** on top of my ice cream.

City There are many tall buildings in the **city**.

Cloud That **cloud** is in the shape of a bluebird.

Couch We ate popcorn on the **couch**.

The Letter D

Desert The **desert** is dry and filled with sand.

Dessert Everyone loves **dessert** after a meal.

Dinner Monkey likes bananas for **dinner**.

Doctor The **doctor** will help you feel better.

Doll My **doll** has red hair.

Dollar I spent one **dollar**.

Eagle The **eagle** flew up and over the trees.

Earth The **Earth** is like a big blue ball.

Easel An **easel** helps hold a painting in place.

Elephant There goes the **elephant** from the circus.

Engine An **engine** makes a car go fast.

Vroom Vroom!

Feast The birds enjoyed a fine **feast**.

Feather A **feather** grows on a bird.

Field The sun is shining on the **field**.

Flower I picked a **flower** just for you.

Forest The **forest** is a quiet and cool place to be.

Fort I wonder who put a flag on that **fort**.

Friend A **friend** is someone you like a lot.

Garden Flowers and plants grow in the **garden**.

Giraffe The **giraffe** is the tallest animal in the world.

Glass Here is a **glass** of water for you.

Grape A **grape** may be red, purple, or green.

Grass A bug creeps through the **grass**.

Guitar Monkey plays his orange **guitar**.

I even take requests!

Hammer A **hammer** is great for hitting nails.

Hand A **hand** has four fingers and a thumb.

Helmet Put on your **helmet** to keep your head safe.

Hill Here is a **hill** that looks fun to climb.

Horse A **horse** eats hay at the end of the day.

House Monkey lives in a big pink **house**.

Swing by some time!

The Letter I

Ice I like to add **ice** to my juice.

Idea An **idea** is a thought that grows in your head.

Igloo An **igloo** has walls made of ice or snow.

Ink I use black **ink** to write a letter.

Island My little **island** has water on all sides.

Ivy That dark green vine is called **ivy**.

Jacket A **jacket** will keep you warm on a cold day.

Juice I want a glass of **juice** for breakfast.

Jungle Monkey plays in the **jungle** all day.

Key Here is the **key** that will open the door.

King The **king** wears a gold crown.

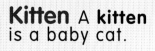

Kitten A **kitten** is a baby cat.

The lion is the king of the jungle!

Ladder I use a **ladder** to climb up high.

Lake We like to run and jump into the **lake**.

Letter I know every **letter** in the alphabet.

Library There are lots of books at the **library**.

And they all taste great!

Lizard A **lizard** likes to get warm in the sun.

Mail I hope I get some **mail** today.

Mask I wonder who is wearing the **mask**.

Math **Math** is my favorite subject.

Meal It is time to eat my **meal**.

Money Here is some **money** to buy bananas.

Moon Sometimes the **moon** makes the night seem bright.

Museum We went to the **museum** to look at the art.

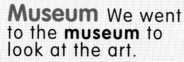

Nail A **nail** is sharp at one end and flat at the other end.

Name Tell me the **name** of that animal.

BAT

Nest There are blue eggs in the **nest**.

Night Every **night** I look at the stars.

Noise That bird made a great big **noise**!

Yowza! That is one loud bird!

Number The **number** two is easy to spell.

Ocean We sailed on the **ocean** for days and days.

Octopus An **octopus** has eight arms and lives in the ocean.

Office An **office** is filled with busy people.

Orchard I picked an apple in the **orchard**.

Ostrich An **ostrich** can run faster than an alligator.

Owl We heard an **owl** hoot late at night.

Park There is a pretty **park** in the middle of town.

Party We ate cake at the **party**.

Peach A **peach** is a very juicy fruit.

Pear Look for a **pear** in that fruit bowl.

Quarter One **quarter** equals twenty-five cents.

I always call "tails," of course.

Radio We danced to songs on the **radio**.

Raft Look at the **raft** floating down the river.

Rainbow I saw a **rainbow** after the storm.

Ribbon The winner receives a big blue **ribbon**.

River The **river** runs into the lake.

Road Follow the monkey that ran down that **road**!

Rope **Rope** is used to pull and tie things.

The Letter S

Sand **Sand** gets hot in the sun.

Sandwich A **sandwich** is good for lunch or dinner.

Seed A plant grows from a very small **seed**.

Stew I am so hungry I could eat six bowls of **stew**!

Summer **Summer** is the best time to play in the sun.

Smells pretty a-peel-ing!

The Letter T

Team We are all members of the same **team**.

GO, PINEAPPLES!

Tent I sleep in a **tent** when I'm camping.

MONKEY-FEST

Ticket Now I have a **ticket** for my favorite show.

Tiger A **tiger** can run, climb, or leap.

Towel I use a **towel** to dry myself off.

Town We went shopping in the big **town**.

The Letter U

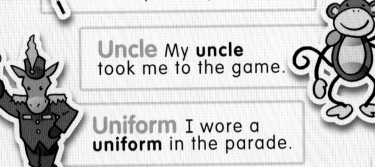

Umbrella This **umbrella** will keep us dry.

Uncle My **uncle** took me to the game.

Uniform I wore a **uniform** in the parade.

The Letter V

Valley I took a walk through the **valley**.

Vase Let's put something pretty in the **vase**.

Village The **village** is next to the lake.

Vine Monkey can swing from **vine** to **vine**.

Voice That is the loudest **voice** I ever heard.

Wagon I like to ride in my red **wagon**.

Walrus Every **walrus** knows how to swim.

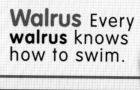

Weather It rained yesterday, but today the **weather** is sunny.

Wind The **wind** is blowing away all the leaves.

And all the monkeys, too!

Window I like to keep the **window** open.

Wood We used **wood** to build a big box.

The Letter X

Xylophone I love to play the **xylophone**.

The Letter Y

Yard Two dogs play in the **yard**.

Yarn **Yarn** is used to knit warm clothes.

Year A **year** is 365 days long.

Yesterday **Yesterday** was my birthday.

Hey! It was mine, too!

Zebra A **zebra** has stripes that are black and white.

Zero **Zero** is another name for nothing.

Zipper My backpack has a big red **zipper**.

Zoo Many kinds of animals live in the **zoo**.